WRITING AIR, WRITTEN WATER

WRITING AIR, WRITTEN WATER

poems by

ROBERTA GOULD

Poems in this collection have appeared in
A Different Drummer, Arete, Best Friends, Buckle, Coop,
Dream Yourself Flying, Group '74, Helicon Nine,
Light: A Poetry Review, Not Guilty, Osiris, Poetry Now,
Pulp, Response, Sunbury, Thirteenth Moon, Twigs, Womansong.

Published in the United States of America
Library of Congress catalog card number 80-81559
ISBN 0-936628-00-6

First edition
Published by Waterside Press
Box 1298 Stuyvesant P.O.
New York 10009, N.Y.

Typography and cover design by Virginia Tan

CONTENTS

I

IV

V

I

AUDUBON'S FLAMINGO

Redder than life
more supple than the S
it thrusts its impossible neck
over the promontory tip
and the tepid waters
which repeat it
in fading birds
that mark the flats
and the haze
Here
so brilliantly feathered
it steps modest and cautious
on raw stilts that reveal
it, too, is flesh
hooked beak near webbed foot ready
keen eyes scanning the shallows
for the flicker of fish

THE CHICK PEAS

Spilled through the funnel
they fall
into the destined bottle
each one revealing
a verse
joined to the next one
lying over and under it
rounds of birth death birth
they tell where they are going
and their dark original home
Listen!
Each common bean of the epic
constellated sings
its secret

YES

Shot a deer
at f 11
1/60th of a second
and brought her back
in the blur of leap
opposing hooves
        midair
and the light of her eyes

Gifted now we gaze at her
and she leaps on
and on

HOUSE

It is unseen
as a leaf falling
in the midst of a forest
but I say
it exists, yes,
as the world outside
my drawn window shade is
I believe.
They try
to talk it away
blow it to the sky
prove again
the blackest horse is white.
I stop my ears
go on seeking
that most substantial house.
Within me they
have become singing
sirens: That is
the most difficult
obstacle. Oh tie me
to my proper wits
I will cast them
from their outposts
in my ear;
rising up to search
with all power
I will discover it.

EXCEPT FOR THIS

Light kindled
in a mirror
facing a window,
sealed
except for an aura
around the dark shade
that does not entirely
cover it
The edges are
glowing air,
silver light
surrendering to the glass
which augments it
like fire risen
The room
        a box
        except for this:
        window obscured
        and its receiving mirror
can't be contained
        Total
dazzle of light
throws back the walls

DOES MUSIC

Does music ride the rails
or burn a path through heaven?
Does it select the highway of its coming?
Is it the process of the road itself?

Sound-form-music-sound
high rising
breaks through me
breaking through
rides the sky out
flowing from itself
beamed across the greyness
as a bridge
to matter's exponential spiral

The auditorium spins off
                                        as light

LISTEN

Listen!
Leaf
on stem
yielding
sings
Wind
cannot
drown out
the thin turning
of its flat green
giving in

RED CLOUD ON LAKE GEORGE

(after an Edward Steichen photograph)

What world is
this apple of a lake
wrinkled in the middle
to the right of silhouette leaves
hanging into the frame
above a cloud
huge as an army
crossing the long black hill
which is a solid wave
that will not break?

and the sky
opened its flaming lips
to admit me
singing

like a long red hearth
the low down
blazing

overwhich
glowed
something

ROSE

It leans in the bottle
opened out its
insides glowing
an arm's length
from the wall
paper that doesn't match
the quilt

Blind to bud
and grooved flower
solid seeming turning
I awake
at the hour
its petals
will fall off

Half withered layers
hang neatly
the day is hot
and slow
nothing moves
we seem
like sculpture

yet I breathe
it live
exhalation
and glance
to the window
where its bush
mates remain

also ready
to leave
their stems
scatter
beside the pond willow

SPECULATIONS

Gilded roses, rabbits frozen
no life no
iris rocking
dervish blown broad ribbon leaf
no dog in pond
hip high
splish splash
and the stream
gurgling on
but stiff shallow breaths
each night numbered
no peace no
sleep away into
undying morning

GONE

I could distill the creek
stir words so
the absence of iris on the bank
seemed better than their being here
last week
Singing I could
call up missing petals
The loss would diminish
even vanish
The rose that set
the marsh on fire
is gone
could say it's blooming yet
but I'll be still no counterfeit
will strain the silence where they stood

MATING BEETLES

Thick armor
doesn't encumber them
clambering over
each other

frenzied upon the few
ungutted leaves
their fury of appetite
has not yet reached

The ravaged tree
holds no sun back
network of veins
without body

Oh insects fierce
may each larva grow
to imago! But let it be
elsewhere, next year

CAT

Freed the cat turns savage in the grass
our city pet who braved apartment walls
becomes the bane of birds, the death of mice

From dawn to dusk he roams the wooded place
will only enter when we call for meals
freed the cat turns savage in the grass

An eerie cachination fills the house
he hears the garden cardinal flash his calls
becomes the bane of birds, the death of mice

springs to the screen and batters for the space
of fifteen minutes till the damned thing falls
freed the cat turns savage in the grass

He claws a mole and almost gets a grouse
defies attempts to tally up his kills
becomes the bane of birds, the death of mice

then disappears all night and who can guess
what ambush he is dreaming as he prowls
freed the cat turns savage in the grass
becomes the bane of birds, the death of mice

II

ELEVEN POEMS
AFTER KANDINSKY IMPROVISATIONS

1

When
whales flew
over leaning castles
that fell east
and off the flat earth
where they drowned in seas
cannon were pushed across
and the sky
was a presage of doom
heaven's green
baring itself
to the flock ranked humbly below
did you notice the peace
of that yellow hill
on the unsettled side of the valley?
Did you see the cloud
signal to go there?
Why didn't you go there?

2

Spires rise
and the hills
gaze up
An egg laughs
in the valley, winks
to the mountain dreaming
the sea revealed
in a conch shell's story
under the musk rose sky
flotilla of yellow
clouds passing

3

The wake of explosion . . .
hard-edged fish triangles
a tailed rhomboid overlapping
two inferred globes
and a monocle hanging
high in the center
pierced by a curved exclamation
come from beyond and trailing
feathered vapors
whose chromatics are heralded
by an advancing flat of rouge
that seems to have nothing
to do with it all

4

An antlered branch
of the circle tree
sings hearts
to the moon
and all the fruits
in paradise rise
and every form of geometry
On a transparent bough
the unborn snow
lies dreaming

5

In the round
within the hand
where three moons
bloom
what tower?
what flower?

6/ LAMENT FOR LOST SKY

A room full of eyes
flocks of gyrating ducks
brilliant elephants
whose legs can see
and ships that are alive
The tongue has not started to click
its way into speech
and heaven still
lies behind the eyes
Then we are told to walk
on our elbows
They set their examples
we strain
and the inner world dims
and the spoon-tapped glass
no longer rings
They talk
We mimic

7/ VOYAGE

I have risen in a basket
        and sing the square stars down
                reach out and grab
      the green one
it wants me to let go
          I let go
      and the tick tack
        takes color
       a straw hat
     and the treble clef
       orbit our vessel
     origami hands
        signal us
     through the cosmic dust
     which is not mapped
        but flashes its code
Then
     through a fogged purple glass
we see music's face
       in the dark
as fleets of lit bridges pass
     winking and humming

8

If the coiffeured madame
got a bit nearer
to the ancient red horse
snorting to the flourish
of the pink lady's clarion
would that ghost of a crow fly away
and leave the philodendron tree?
Would the cluster of flowers
pinned to her waist
become a spider and slide off?
In her organdy gown she leans
extending her arms
like a canopy
over each mythic animal
on that blue pasture
But the halo of an enormous tulip
gives better umbrage
The yellow sky seeps
back to earth
and everything hums

A wedge of golden melon
in a spiraling garden
of raspberries

Indigo strings
announcing the harp's
new year

The sun rising huge
lines of migrating birds
abandoning winter
unwilling to smash
on the castle's red
ramparts, once more

10

The tulip has left its stem
flown up to the burgundy river
where a parakeet's dream
tips its wing
and blue rocks orbit their hill

But killers scowl through the hedges
and a dead branch resembles a gun
The pink rain doesn't cure me
I've been poisoned
It lingers in the blood

Yet I go on – sun shards
pierce the clouds
and fireworks explode
under the new year's funnel
bringing smiles even to *my* face

I'm going to study egg yolks
I'm going to swim through the wall
where the headstone winks
aware that no soul
has ever been buried beneath it

My eyes which are your mirrors,
shadow-faced, gloved torturers,
won't go blind up there
where the mist goes
and red is the glory of your extinction

11

The sun has wings
which three high hoops witness
Pastel streamers celebrate this
A green railing
near dreamed Venus
curves with its long echo
orbiting the moon of her moon
It's really a happy kitchen
Each worm in the cabbage
is joyous
Each saw-toothed form
smiles freely
Even the question mark shimmers
flexed to new functions
On the fluid staircase
an eel sings
accompanied by fruit
configured in the polychrome sweep
of music's new clef
If you wish to dance
the collapsible stage
put on your mock moustache
and hold the strings tightly
We'll say the globes are balloons
and you the anchor of their universe
or when you sleep
that the floor rises to give praise
under the green banner of exhilaration

III

JULY NOTES

Because the price of wash went up
I took it five blocks down the street
to do myself

As it spun I
wrote a morning
                    after
                  poem
to you away
and nodded
              elbow pressed to table
words down
              one by one
In state of love when done
              returning to the laundry
I smiled and filled that figure
waiting on the bench
with joy
innocent of "you" or "I"

and dreamed of writing air
and written water

VOYEUSE

I spied you out
from the heights
awaiting your appearance
moon face

Three hours ebbed
you arrived
turning into the channel
of Ninth Street
I raised my field glasses
gazed

That was all . . .
like fishing
or waiting with camera
for the bird to return to its nest

calm all the while
on that roof
grown tan
in the slow summer sun
that set behind the building
where you passed

MUSICIAN

I bought her an organ
with a fraction of my treasure
and lifted her to herself
as once they said
only the gods could

I acquired the face of destiny
power turning to heart
mother giving unrestrictedly
knowing no division

And the music came
playing her gifted
she sat on her tuffet
a constellated waterfall
I hid behind the firmament and listened

CAPITAL LOVE

fell
along with the other
commodities
at the time
of the devaluation
which stood for
losing the war
which was their
control of the world
slipping

What do you have
to do with all that?
Tell me.
Why so scarce
when it is your spirit
which does not end
like money?

SONG FOR LAZARILLO DE TORMES

oh white oh white flower
silver tasseled
  tossed
corn carted into the mill

oh white oh white flower
silver corn of morning
box cars to the mill at last
grain filched no more

oh white oh white flower
silver tasseled
  tossed
corn carted into the mill

SWITCH

Under the brim of your hat
I grow distant
Wearing my socks
you approach
We trade names
carry each other's package
At the airport
someone embarks
someone stays
in the tower
waving
There's no telling
who is who
The take-off goes well

LEFT

The suddenly empty room,
still ringing,
and your half drained glass
on the piano
as I dizzy, sweat and fall away,
suggest I had you once,
absence calling presence up.
And yet I cannot break
the axis of the wheel
to distance free as one
looking into light in bliss
or in the flames pronouncing love
No!
Attached as always
I am the walls that kept you here,
and quake, that the door
has let you out
for good.

ATTACK

In two
the organ
split apart
warring cleaved
pressed hard
till pain prevailing
won the day
gall's legions
spilled
to far dominions
up the back
and at the heart
of breath

What one
could not
the opposites
staked their flag
of claim on
the body stopped
its functioning
that afternoon
the splendid August sun
remained
unseen

TAMPERING

Like a rose
your poem
plucked from air

stamped
and presented
with your name
and fanfare

bloomed of its own
accord
but now become
a token
of you

not needed
why don't you
wear it in your hair
thrust it through the neck
of a porcelain jar

your work
bound tight, sure
and fixed
as the promise of death . . .
your very own, secure

DYNAMICS

There's a roomful of people
and the man with the loudest voice
asserts the moon
is not white
They either agree or
mildly offer alternatives
which he promptly refutes
putting each dissenter in his place

Then all compete to agree
but too many vie
for his favor
so a portion spills over
to the couch to win
the approval of his friend
the cowboy who lounges there

They bring out the cards
do push ups
have a rousing time
Up in the attic
you can hear their guffawing
till suddenly the door slams
all the windows rattle
and you wonder what whim
takes them to what saloon
or if they are out
with their shotguns
hunting squirrels again

COMPETITORS

They do not conspire
for your happiness
They cast lots
for your space
speak
where your voice was
gouged out
and they helped

PUPPY

Like any matter
between her teeth
the *Odyssey*
was a rag
to shake
fiercely.
Fragments strewn
on the floor
were evidence
of her delight.
What hero, siren,
cyclops, god,
had ever entered
that house?
a sheer mess
and hard
to sweep,
her quivering
mass of fur
charging the broom
as rebuke came
but did not echo
and, somewhere,
across the room,
a muffled
laugh.

IT CAME

Your words
tight springs
possessed us
right left
right left
tin soldiers
we marched

The ground
claimed was
old world
absolute it
exploded
under us

Agape we
lay tongueless

the walls fell
thick
we quaked

Later much later
the waves
the wreckage
receded

HUGE

Huge you go
that being all
no end

Taller than roof
lidded system
you can't be held
by the house
it bursts

sky open then
your body containing
enters

not striding
tight and fierce
though towards the sun
beyond sun

and windows blew out
walls fell back
wind danced wild possession

as day blazed
and your footprints vanished
over the hill

AN ANCIENT SCROLL

Kyoto burning
    waves of soldiers
        fleeing
A rush from the pavillion
        rows of bodies
            over hedges
             leaping
                   off the edge
         observing
       I stand
a thousand years ahead

their burning eyes

IT

To pluck
that star
from the horizon
I thrust my hand
through the frame
The sky crumbles
I pull out
the twisted arms
of a galaxy
that once
turned and burned
This proves something
The hole in the picture
is a constant reminder
of IT

IV

FACE

Like a moon crater
or an abandoned salt flat
that mouth in defeat
under the furrows of a brow rising
like an encephalograph needle
recording all but understanding
nothing those eyes won't tell
gone dull and unable to cry
in their rigid sockets

DREAM

A huge roach bead-bottomed
and supernaturally large,
winged past my eyes
in a place of deep relaxation,
where leaders lurking
cast their nets,
emerged from behind cash registers,
is a new Pegasus rising.
Now all I have to do is
shrink a little more,
then I'll be able to mount
the creature, ride,
and inhabit the air
of this new age,
an absolute angel.

When the leaders return
to their checkout counters
and the buzz of wings ceases,
workaday Monday back again,
I line up as my neighbors do
and trembling wait
to exchange my body
for the meat in the bag,
stooping as they ring us up,
slipping quietly out.

DREAM 67

In the foot shallow water, over the linoleum,
no gilled thing is swimming
where boats are moored to beds
and you're lucky to be rented anything

They will not let the vessels out
have sealed the doors to the bay
agreeing to accept
the flooded room as a sea

Pay gladly
    though the fishing is nil
    cheats win
    and all names have been switched
    forcing the day
you clearly recognize death's rig
and living walk away

WHAT NAME

Roman horses stir in their molds
Stylized tails quiver
Another parade is readied below
They go round

The page, a fragment of cylinder, turns
Notes bellowed resound
Lyrics rise from their long throats
Move the procession on

Or are they lions
That double series
Contrapuntal
Spaced in the middle?

What's what?
And who is who?

When you read me
What name do you dream?
When I dream you
Who writes the poem?

MONDAY MORNING

Dawn comes
the world's procedure
is dumped
on the fearful sleeper
who dreams
to a dull awakening
unremembered depths
sealed off
business
the order
of the morning star

THE SIGNAL

We grab the sheets
and dash across the lawn
They are standing on the steps
to a porch near an airport
The yellow sky
suddenly swoops down
Granite urns
line the green
contain invisible hounds
that pursue us
as crickets hoist flags
and the flowers form squadrons
This is jet lag
Your scream
like a fishbone
sticks in my throat
my blood's journey stops

A pair of empty gloves
called "the controller"
signals us on
through the sulphuric fog

AFTER HIERONYMUS BOSCH

Doom looms
in the doorway
around the corner
demons lurk
They close in
and pounce
ride you wild
over the hump
whip you up frenzied
You shriek
shield your eyes
and cower
seek rock
to crawl under
they are not
unfamiliar yet
you are in terror
Then all join in
and ring you round
grimace as they
mock the sun
You succumb to them
and are not refused
They devour you then
oh my
good
woman

FIRST MOON LANDING

July 16, 1969

So what! The dark side of the moon's on view
and mystery's been pushed to reason's gate
we flare as hounds or wild cypress might

And images seen surfaced, safe and known,
touched, clutched, cherished, leaned upon,
sink as sand mirrors with the rising tide

as bobbing gulls at rest are buoyed beneath
a sky that's ever present now that luck
has lifted it with moving iron hook

Yet top or bottom, front or rear won't show
the universe contingent upon now . . .
its temporary absolute that kills

THE DEPARTURE

Limousine
third in a series of birds
flashes by
Behind his bullet proof glass
the governor crouches low
head oversized &
shining
like the rump
of a hog

Left
with a bag full
of book ends
a bottle and purse
along with the door-stop
and other practical aids
to high living
I
stanchion
take in the vision

He plucks a ball of feathers from his coffee
and shatters to ten thousand skies

IT PERSISTS

I'm tired!
The same duplicity
smiling
believing itself
innocent
has managed to butcher
the cat
You walk off
with a neat package
bakery string around
the white waxed paper
and I remain
in what I thought
was a fishstore
I watched
as John ran his thumb
down Fat Grey's throat
which sent her
into raptures of sleep
but I did not catch on
Toothpaste arrived
in the mail
relatives
were united
at death beds
your mother
impatiently paced

the street
as I gazed absently
then suddenly
saw you take
the package
and knew in a flash
and was lost
My words
became rags
your brown teeth
and the light
in your eyes
looking up at me
seemed to be
asking for love
I thought you
were going to curtsey
Later, as I slept,
a spoon was placed
in my mouth
and I woke
with an acrid taste
that would not
go away
I've tried all
the toothpaste
It persists

3 POEMS AFTER PAUL KLEE PAINTINGS

1. TYRANT

When your face fell off
and your forehead split open
leaving your eyes intact
though you could not see
past your brow
half gone like a forest cleaved
where new highways run,
when your chin flattened
to hold on to the table
mouth set straight in unhappiness
like a wired mannequin,
I wanted to put you together
but when I reached out to touch you
I remembered you mocking their deaths.
I stopped my hand then
telling my heart, "Be Still.
Control yourself."

2. AMATEUR DRUMMER

Musicians gone
I parade around
the stage
all my own
BONG BONG
my legs
do not trip me
the moving
kettle drum
high as a table
receiving
the rapturous raps
of these fists
extended with sticks
to sound the dome
of the hall
I've entered
this noon
I almost reach
heaven
beating my
untrained heart out
knowing I fail
to bring grace
to the air
THUMP THUMP
striking the roof
echoing dull

3. FIGURES

The shadow grows pale
when its host veers west
and struts mightily off
lifting its transparent cape
to let it sit
white on its knee
decisively lifting and falling
in its march to the edge of the canvas

And like an avatar's angel
a black figure also hovers
pointing the way
wrapped round its neck
and turning grey as we look
through the head of its master
which has no substance
and is the head of a ghost

COMMUNICATION

The wired air
intercepting us
shrieks

Better submerge
and try other signalling
words fail

or beyond the stratosphere
forget it
and float with the asteroids

INTERRUPTION

Interruption of beads
A knot in the necklace
Gap between halves
They can't slide across
It defies them
They can't slide at all
No flow
And the circle
broken

POEM IN THREE SCENES

Elongating the bones with a grease pencil
he leans over each time a skull
is perceived on the plains
though it really is a ball
rolled to a stop in Flatbush . . .
not that death is ignored
not that living blocks vision
of the skeletons that bear us

And the day dawns fogged, soft, intimate,
We come in groups to a sewer grating
it's a festival. . . an ancient woman
calls up the snakes we have waited for
The weather helps, and her quiet song,
Everywhere serpents surface and cause wonder

When the light grows subtle, quick, an hour later,
two women pass each other weight wise
The fat one's body shrinks, is a twig-like structure,
the thin one inflates to where the other one was
Become each other in the grosser features of form
they see then through each other's eyes

FOUR SCENES
IN ASCENDING PROGRESSION

I

She is marooned
on her own island
and receives no word
Ships sail past
but she cannot sound
through their great steam blasts
that warn the little craft
that are not there
to take warning

II

She is lost
in the dome of sound
throws up her arms
but is not seen on the screen

III

Invisible mute
she is under a sky of first
light the waters
spark there is no
gory beast there
the new age is
empty of murder

IV

She leaps across

V

IN MEMORY OF MARIANNE MOORE

"I thank you. . . that you approve
of my efforts, which are often useless" —MM

I

The slow snow
on the same street
as night falls
falls as flakes
of dandruff
purple in glare
of street lamp
harsh in fluorescence
and fact

II

This is the window
where she sat
gathering up her nerve
to sing alone
as the mad might
those songless days
of suicide
crawling hatred circling home
the war at last begun

III

Elegant, deft,
noble in gift
she served

when living claimed
her voice
as others set the tone,
fashion, diversion,
with hieratic sneers
and smiling fiddle
in the arrogant name of art

IV

City of hatred
city of the free
who'll damage all
the lack of stars allows
lay her cold frame to rest
beneath your streets
driving on
to pleasure, food and fun

The times are prosperous
if you are rich
the day's a good one
if you frame your feet
and never look beyond
or linger on
the past
or unseen land
your brothers bomb

V

She was finally weary
and useless as always
in all but fire
and spirit
which last
beyond the crumbling
of these towers
growled prayers
go forth from
up their piece of sky

–Brooklyn, N.Y. 1972

EVELYN DEAD

On the organs
of her body palace
they feed

airy lung piles
light as manna

liver blood pools
to lap

the still heart
pure morsel
for solemn feasting

Mites!
She sustains you
now as then . . .
that big woman

EYES

The earth crouching arcs its spine
and the sun rises over a ridge
huge face the mountain lifts

into the sky where emptiness is
and a hand urges it up
At the tree line a dog sits

guarding morning's wedge of the world
beneath which calm beetles burrow
and shine for no one at all

next to a head bereft of eyes
that bares the white of its skull
to the stones and the seeds

SYLVIA

Death has taken that woman
out of the realm of candied sweets
canaries, terriers, cousins.
She has gone down where her mother is
The quiet county takes her back

Oh sacred hole, bloom fast!
Make be what couldn't come
flowering here breathe again
In new spruce, fir, forsythia
Say she lives

THE MESSAGE AFTER

"en mi tu voz, voz viva"
for Pedro Garfias

The beauty of death is
always becoming love
progression past eye speed
up the body cracking
saying, "Look what I augur
young blood
Go!
I give my bones back now
walk the earth lightly

And when the grass
returns
remember to remember
me lion-fierce
at terminal
to fare you off well
daughter
of my eyes
one globe
this torture
you go to

And may you take my knowing out
as contagion of song
to the loss-plagued century isthmus
I walk unarmed
as my mane
flag of moons
glows for the last time
signalling you
to take this poem
as a seed of peace
as I go"

REVISIT / OAXACA DEATH MASK

Angular crystal skull
Suddenly seen
And a voice like an echo
Drifting out to me
Faceless now I
Know you blazing in jelly
Or born of the microwave sky
Our latest legacy
Death as in ancient times
Delivers its mask
And now you come out
In dignity
Stand in the doorway
Hold it before you
And speak
From that other time
The space between your flesh
And the lucid stone signifies

And I can only guess
Your missing face
Beneath that pass to the world
Art carves for you in its mercy
Whether there is nothing at all
To show beneath it
Or whether everything's there
But for a lip
Cleft with its palate
Some such singularity
I do not know
Yet honor the secret
As in those other times
When death was deity
I listen to your voice
That comes from somewhere
And thank you, Mixteca, for reaching me

GHOST

The air scooped
holds its trace
and form
The winds rush in
and sound

STILL LIFE

In memory of Ree Dragonette

Strips of snow
on a sea of sand
like bars
where old ships foundered
Against the frozen harbor
sky
an immobile shoal
of rushes
And one stark tree
whose branches flare

PATTERNS ON A WINTER AFTERNOON

The sharp winter twigs
are the first fence of my dreams
The world is a haze
beyond that bramble of things
the skaters a blur
thick padded bodies
caught with a leg off the ice
arms extended to balance
the rising ground
or to lift and heave it
back to the sky . . .
soft black forms
crossing the frame

FLYING

Fetters fall off you
dream yourself flying
It is!
and you sing
thanks to hands
soar
and bear the cloud tidings
No rest you
visit the caves
of unborn snow
tend the rain's seedlings
never forget
your dreary beginnings
bondage you break from
rising high
over the next country

LIVING SPACE

When the body is flattened
and folded back with the bed
at the advent of clock change
and vanishes into the couch
you can bet your moon it's time.
Yes. But there's no need to cry
"I'm crushed," even though
the coils press
just sing out like a good ghost
and when the cushions
muffle your voice
Sing louder.